AF188404

Impressum
Verlag: BABADADA GmbH, Nedderfeld 112 , 22529 Hamburg
Geschäftsführer / Verlagsleitung: Harald Hof
Druck: Books on Demand GmbH, In de Tarpen 42, 22848 Norderstedt

Imprint
Publisher: BABADADA GmbH, Nedderfeld 112 , 22529 Hamburg, Germany
Managing Director / Publishing direction: Harald Hof
Print: Books on Demand GmbH, In de Tarpen 42, 22848 Norderstedt

1

escuela

classroom
aula

divide
dividir

186/2

board
mesa

school yard
patio de escuela

teacher
docente

paper
papel

write
escribir

pen
bolígrafo

desk
escritorio

ruler
regla

book
libro

pupil
alumno

satchel

mochila escolar

pencil case

caja de lápices

pencil

lápiz

pencil sharpener

sacapuntas

rubber

goma de borrar

drawing pad

bloc de dibujo

drawing

dibujo

paintbrush

pincel

paint box

caja de pinturas

scissors

tijera

glue

pegamento

exercise book

libro de ejercicios

homework

tarea

number

número

add

sumar

subtract

restar

multiply

multiplicar

calculate

calcular

letter

letra

alphabet

alfabeto

word

palabra

text	read	chalk
texto	leer	tiza
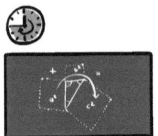		
lesson	register	examination
lección	libro de clase	examen

certificate	school uniform	education
certificado	uniforme escolar	educación

encyclopedia	university	microscope
enciclopedia	universidad	microscopio
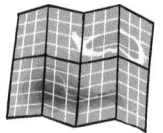		
map	waste-paper basket	
mapa	cesto de papeles	

travel
viaje

hotel
hotel
Grand
hostel
albergue
ROOMS
currency exchange office
casa de cambio
car
auto

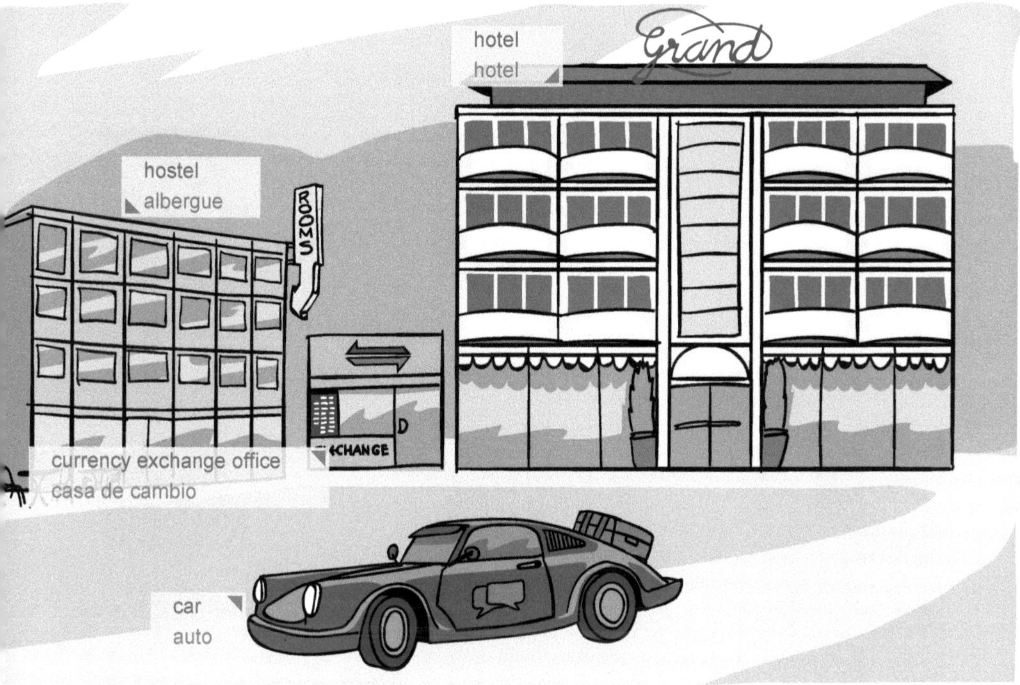

language
idioma

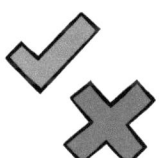

yes / no
sí / no

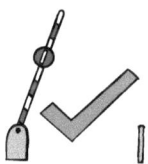

Okay
ok

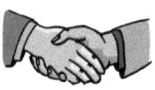

hello
hola

translator
intérprete

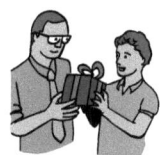

Thank you
gracias

how much is...?

¿Cuánto cuesta...?

I don´t get it

No entiendo

problem

problema

Good evening!

¡Buenas tardes!

Good morning!

¡Buenos días!

Good night!

¡Buenas noches!

goodbye

adiós

direction

dirección

luggage

equipaje

bag

bolso

backpack

mochila

guest

invitado

room

cuarto

sleeping bag

saco de dormir

tent

tienda de campaña

travel - viaje

tourist information

información al turista

beach

playa

credit card

tarjeta de crédito

breakfast

desayuno

lunch

almuerzo

dinner

cena

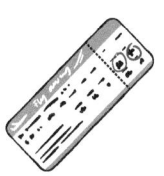

Ticket

pasaje

elevator

ascensor

stamp

sello

border

límite

customs

aduana

embassy

embajada

visa

visa

passport

pasaporte

travel - viaje

transport
transporte

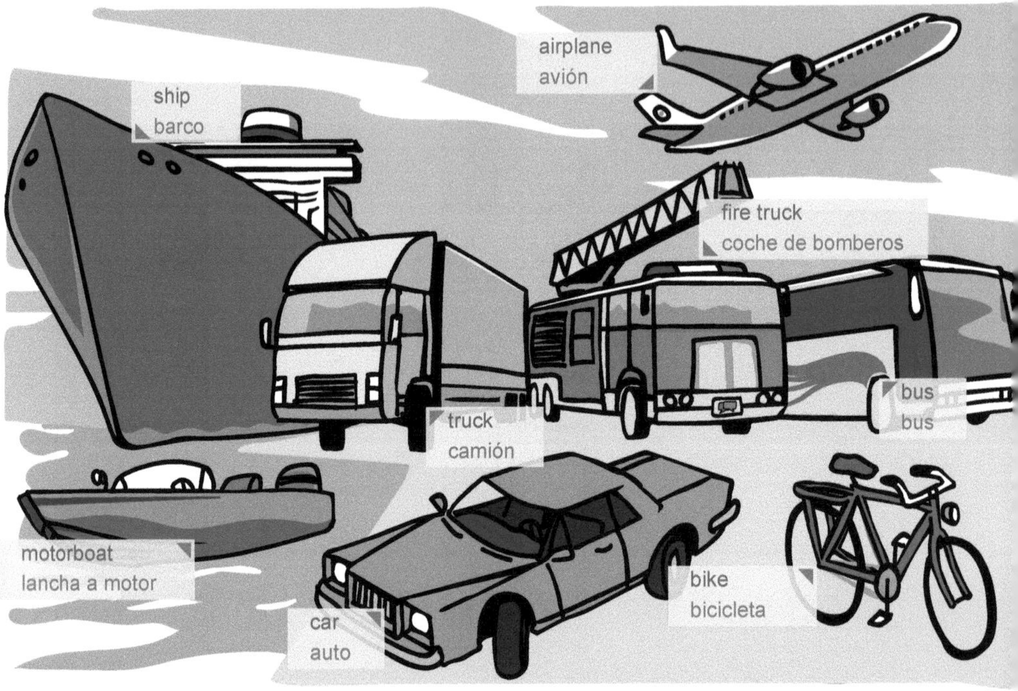
airplane
avión
ship
barco
fire truck
coche de bomberos
bus
bus
truck
camión
motorboat
lancha a motor
bike
bicicleta
car
auto

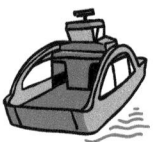

ferry

balsa

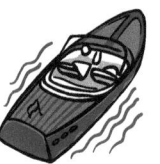

boat

lancha

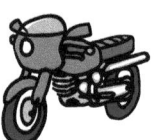

motorbike

motocicleta

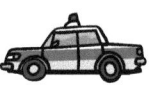

police car

auto de policía

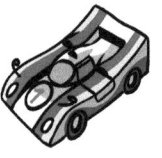

racing car

auto de carreras

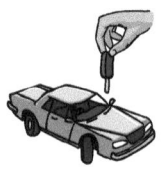

rental car

auto de alquiler

car sharing

alquiler de autos

tow truck

grúa

garbage truck

vehículo recolector de basura

engine

motor

fuel

gasolina

fuel station

gasolinera

traffic sign

señal de tráfico

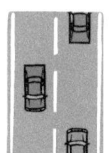

traffic

tránsito

traffic jam

atasco

parking lot

estacionamiento

train station

estación de tren

tracks

carril

train

tren

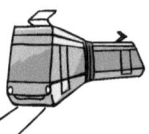

tram

tranvía

wagon

vagón

helicopter

helicóptero

airport

aeropuerto

tower

torre

passenger

pasajero

container

contenedor

carton

caja de cartón

cart

carro

basket

cesta

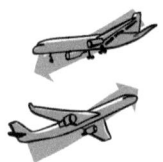

take off / land

despegar / aterrizar

city

ciudad

village

aldea

city center

centro de la ciudad

house

casa

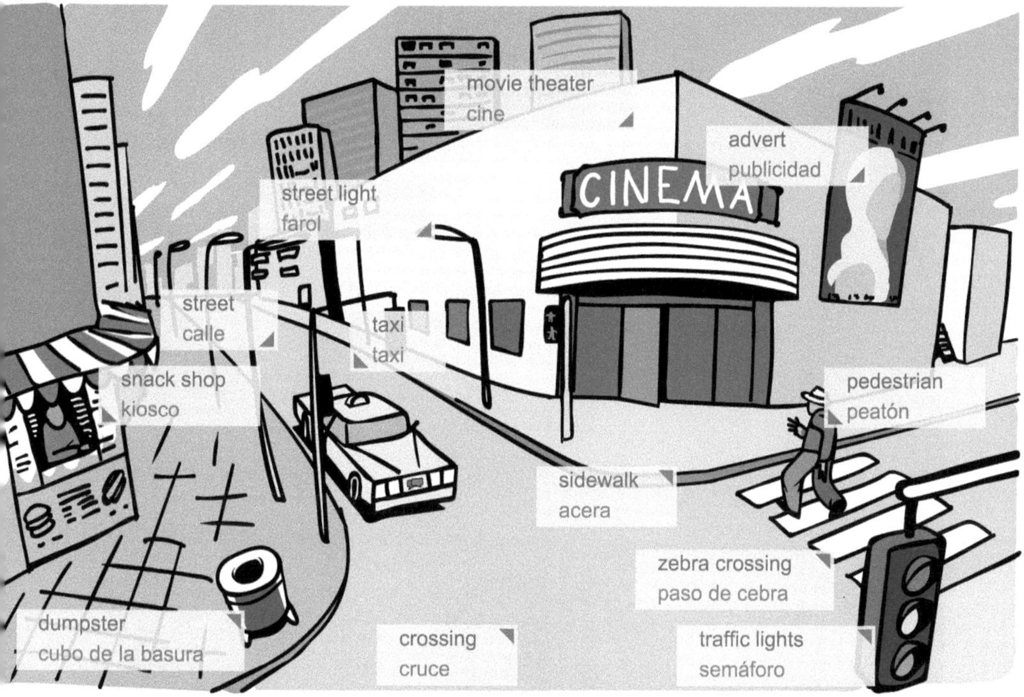

movie theater
cine

advert
publicidad

street light
farol

street
calle

taxi
taxi

snack shop
kiosco

pedestrian
peatón

sidewalk
acera

zebra crossing
paso de cebra

dumpster
cubo de la basura

crossing
cruce

traffic lights
semáforo

CINEMA

hut
cabaña

apartment
apartamento

train station
estación de tren

city hall
ayuntamiento

museum
museo

MUSEUM

school
escuela

city - ciudad

university	bank	hospital
universidad	banco	hospital

hotel	pharmacy	office
hotel	farmacia	oficina

book shop	shop	flower shop
librería	negocio	florería

supermarket	market	department store
supermercado	mercado	grandes almacenes

fishmonger's shop	mall	harbor
pescadería	centro comercial	puerto

park

parque

bench

banco

bridge

puente

stairs

escalera

subway

metro

tunnel

túnel

bus stop

parada de autobuses

bar

bar

restaurant

restaurante

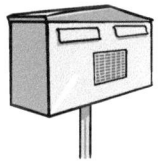

postbox

buzón de correo

street sign

letrero

parking meter

parquímetro

zoo

zoológico

swimming pool

piscina

mosque

mezquita

farm
granja

pollution
polución

cemetery
cementerio

church
iglesia

playground
parque infantil

temple
templo

landscape

paisaje

signpost
indicador de camino

path
sendero

meadow
pradera

stone
piedra

hiker
caminante

tree
árbol

river
río

grass
pasto

flower
flor

valley

valle

hill

montaña

lake

lago

forest

bosque

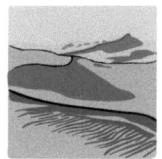

desert

desierto

volcano

volcán

castle

castillo

rainbow

arco iris

mushroom

seta

palm tree

palmera

mosquito

mosquito

fly

mosca

ant

hormiga

bee

abeja

spider

araña

beetle

escarabajo

frog

rana

squirrel

ardilla

hedgehog

erizo

hare

liebre

owl

lechuza

bird

pájaro

swan

cisne

boar

jabalí

deer

ciervo

moose

alce

dam

embalse

wind turbine

aerogenerador

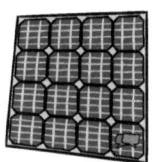

solar panel

módulo solar

climate

clima

restaurant
restaurante

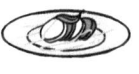

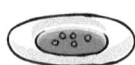

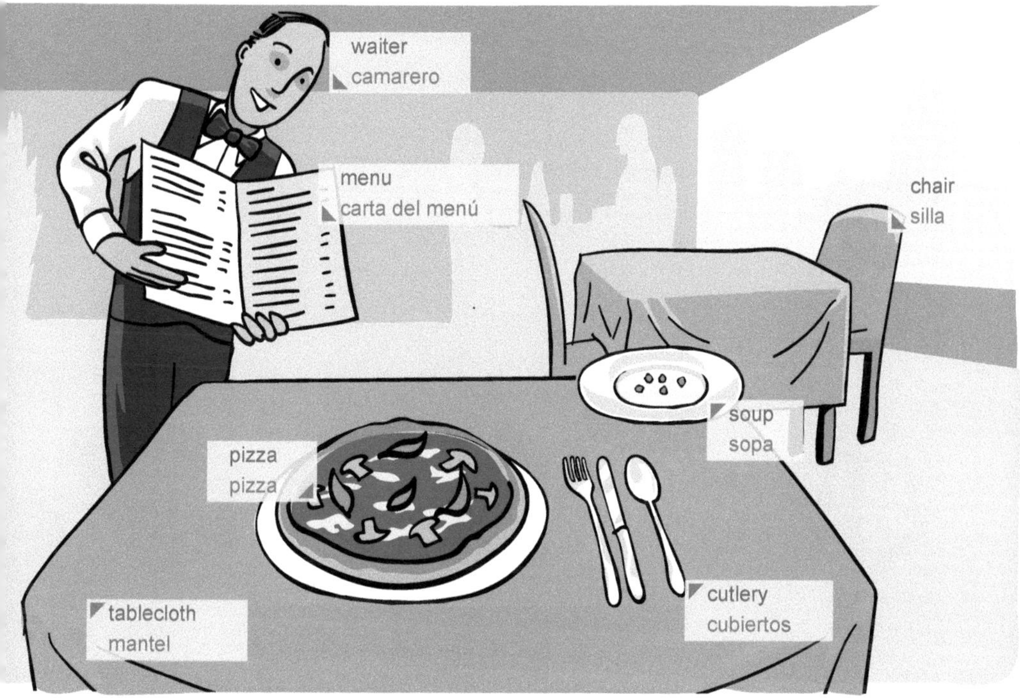
waiter
camarero
menu
carta del menú
chair
silla
soup
sopa
pizza
pizza
tablecloth
mantel
cutlery
cubiertos

starter

entrada

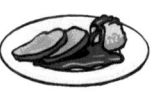

main course

plato principal

dessert

postre

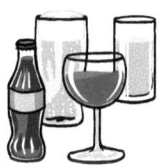

drinks

bebida

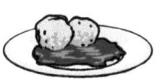

food

comida

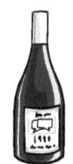

bottle

botella

fast food

comida rápida

street food

comida callejera

teapot

tetera

sugar bowl

azucarera

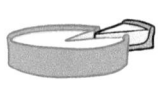

portion

porción

espresso machine

máquina de espresso

high chair

silla alta

bill

factura

tray

bandeja

knife

cuchillo

fork

tenedor

spoon

cuchara

teaspoon

cuchara de té

serviette

servilleta

glass

vaso

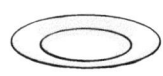

plate

plato

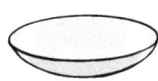

soup plate

plato de sopa

saucer

platillo

sauce

salsa

salt shaker

salero

pepper mill

molinillo para pimienta

vinegar

vinagre

oil

aceite

spices

especias

ketchup

ketchup

mustard

mostaza

mayonnaise

mayonesa

supermarket

supermercado

special offer
oferta
FOR
customer
cliente
dairy products
productos lácteos
fruit
fruta
shopping cart
carrito de compras

BUTCHERS

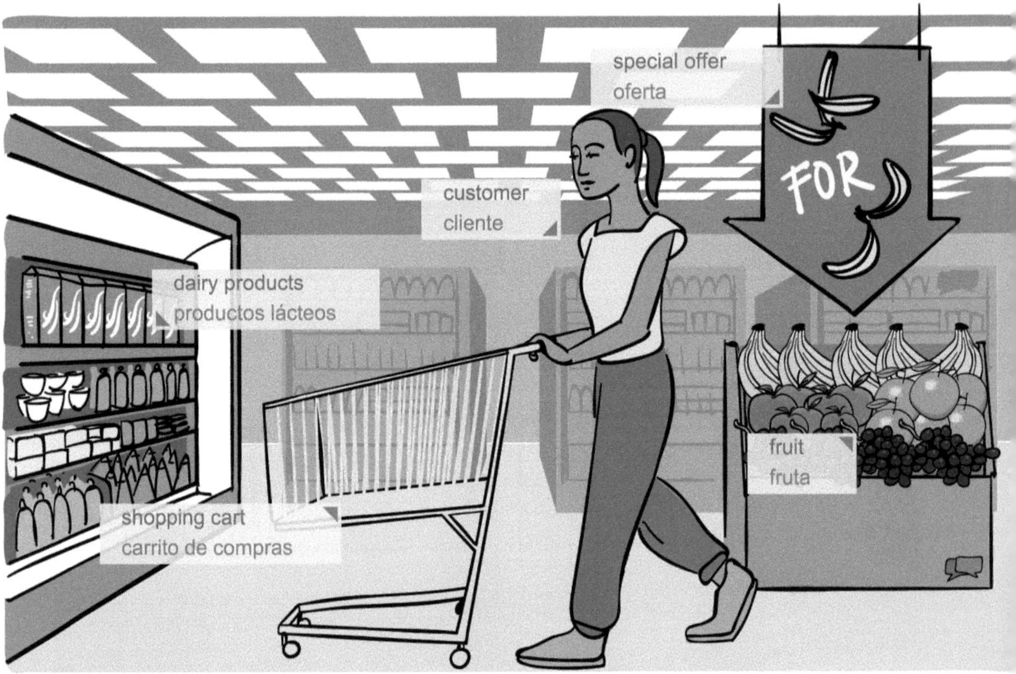

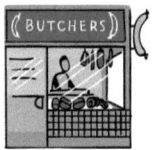

butcher's shop

carnicería

BAKERY

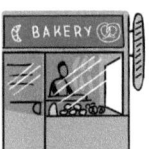

bakery

panadería

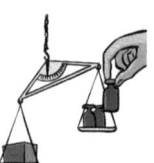

weigh

pesar

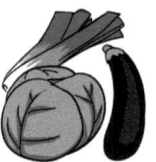

vegetables

verdura

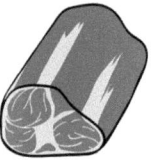

meat

carne

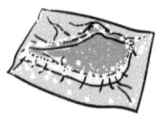

frozen food

alimentos congelados

cold cuts

fiambre

canned food

conservas

detergent

detergente en polvo

candy

dulces

household products

artículos domésticos

cleaning products

productos de limpieza

sales representative

vendedora

cash register

caja

cashier

cajero

shopping list

lista de compras

opening hours

horario de atención

wallet

cartera

credit card

tarjeta de crédito

bag

maleta

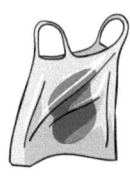

plastic bag

bolsa plástica

water

agua

juice

jugo

milk

leche

coke

refresco de cola

wine

vino

beer

cerveza

alcohol

alcohol

cocoa

cacao

tea

té

coffee

café

espresso

espresso

cappuccino

cappuccino

banana

banana

apple

manzana

orange

naranja

melon

sandía

lemon

limón

carrot

zanahoria

garlic

ajo

bamboo

bambú

onion

cebolla

mushroom

seta

nuts

nueces

noodles

fideos

spaghetti

espagueti

rice

arroz

salad

ensalada

fries

patatas fritas

fried potatoes

patatas salteadas

pizza

pizza

hamburger

hamburguesa

sandwich

sándwich

escalope

escalope

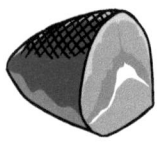

ham

jamón

salami

salame

sausage

embutido

chicken

pollo

roast

asado

fish

pescado

food - comida

porridge oats

copos de avena

muesli

musli

cornflakes

copos de maíz tostado

flour

harina

croissant

croissant

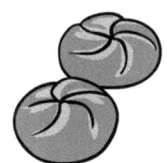

bread roll

panecillo

bread

pan

toast

tostada

cookies

galletas

butter

mantequilla

curd

cuajada

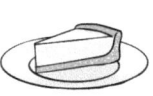

cake

pastel

egg

huevo

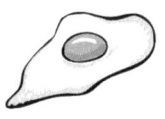

fried egg

huevo frito

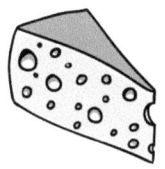

cheese

queso

ice cream

helado

sugar

azúcar

honey

miel

jelly

mermelada

nougat cream

praliné

curry

curry

farm
granja

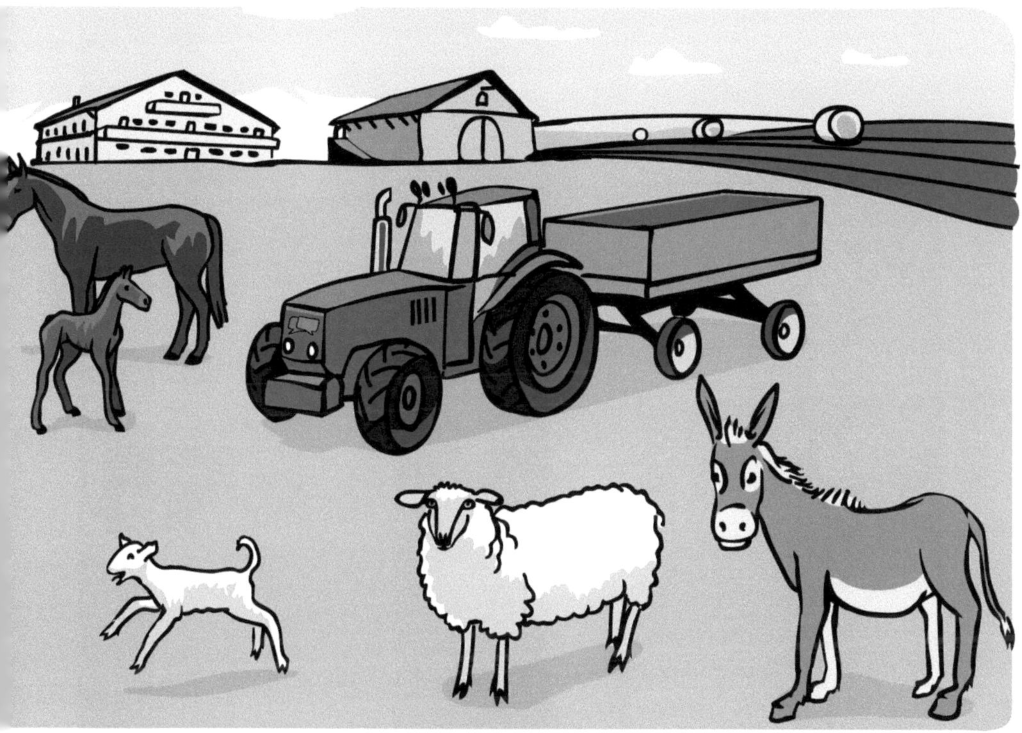

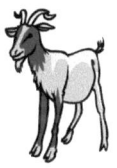

goat

cabra

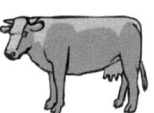

cow

vaca

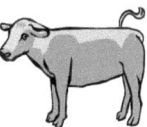

calf

ternero

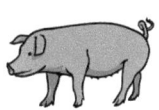

pig

cerdo

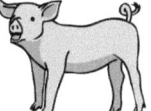

piglet

lechón

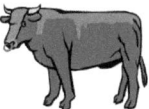

bull

toro

goose

ganso

duck

pato

chick

polluelo

hen

pollo

cockerel

gallo

rat

rata

cat

gato

mouse

ratón

ox

buey

dog

perro

dog house

caseta del perro

garden hose

manguera de riego

watering can

regadera

scythe

guadaña

plow

arado

sickle

hoz

hoe

azada

pitchfork

bieldo

axe

hacha

pushcart

carretilla

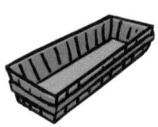

trough

abrevadero

milk can

lechera

sack

saco

fence

cerca

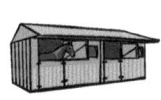

stable

establo

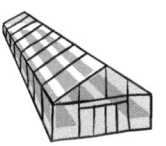

greenhouse

invernadero

soil

suelo

seed

semilla

fertilizer

fertilizante

combine harvester

cosechadora

harvest

cosechar

harvest

cosecha

yams

raíz de ñame

wheat

trigo

soya

soja

potato

patata

corn

maíz

rapeseed

colza

fruit tree

Árbol frutal

manioc

mandioca

grain

cereales

house
casa

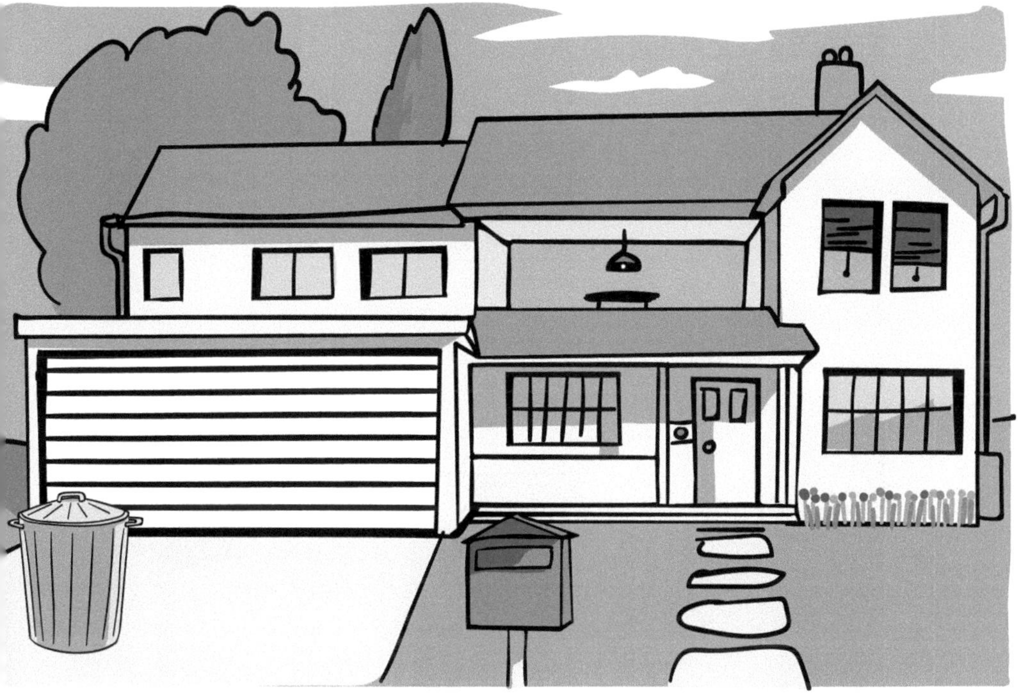

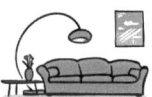

living room

cuarto de estar

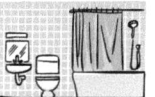

bathroom

cuarto de baño

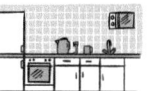

kitchen

cocina

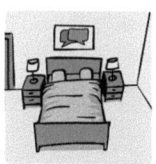

bedroom

dormitorio

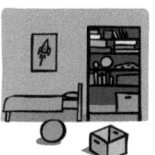

kids room

cuarto de los niños

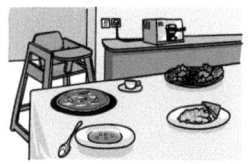

dining room

comedor

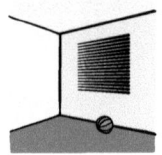

floor

piso

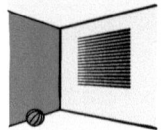

wall

pared

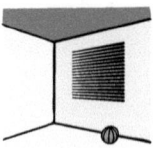

ceiling

cielorraso

cellar

sótano

sauna

sauna

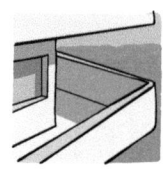

balcony

balcón

terrace

terraza

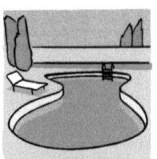

pool

piscina

lawn mower

cortacésped

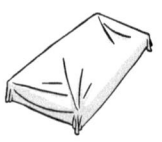

sheet

funda nórdica

bedspread

edredón

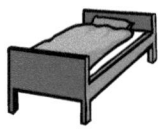

bed

cama

broom

escoba

bucket

cubo

switch

interruptor

living room
cuarto de estar

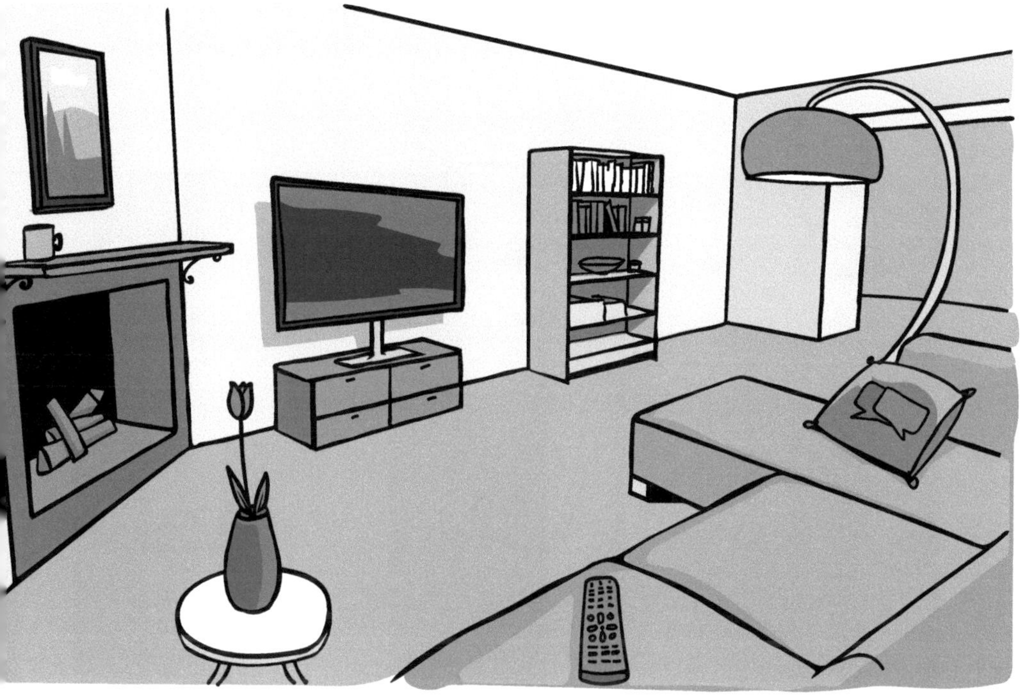

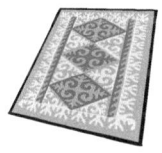

carpet
alfombra

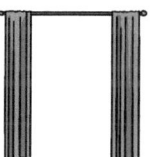

drape
cortina

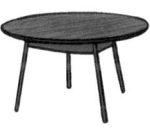

table
mesa

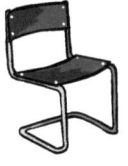

chair
silla

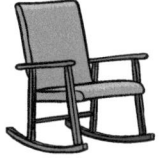

rocking chair
mecedora

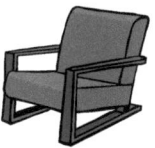

armchair
sillón

book

libro

blanket

frazada

decoration

decoración

firewood

leña

film

film

stereo system

equipo estereofónico

key

llave

newspaper

periódico

painting

cuadro

poster

póster

radio

radio

notebook

bloc de notas

vacuum cleaner

aspiradora

cactus

cactus

candle

vela

kitchen
cocina

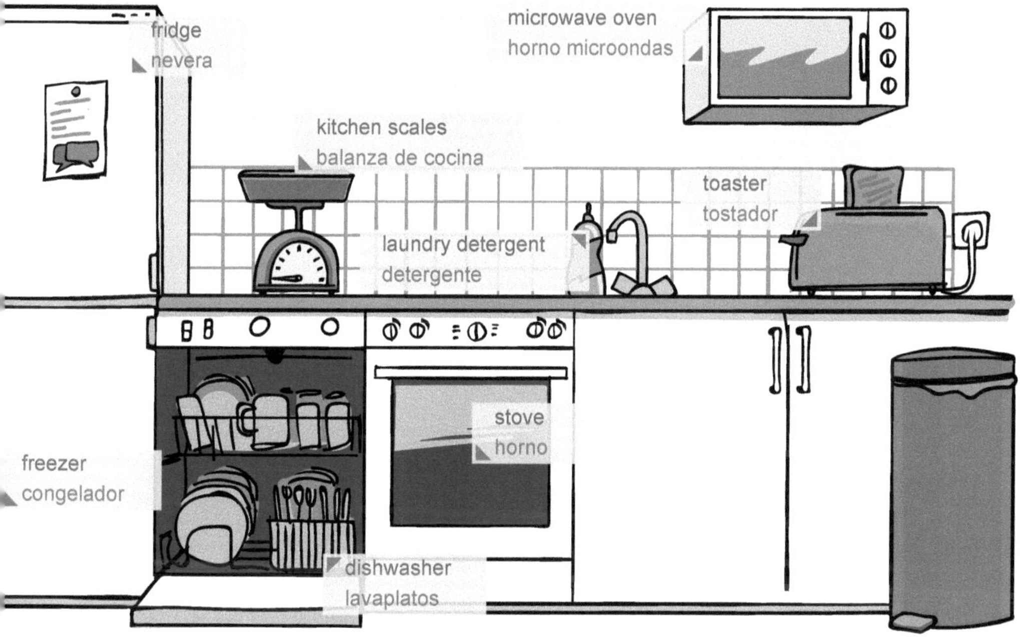
fridge
nevera
microwave oven
horno microondas
kitchen scales
balanza de cocina
toaster
tostador
laundry detergent
detergente
stove
horno
freezer
congelador
dishwasher
lavaplatos

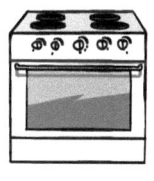

cooker
cocina

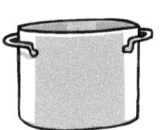

pot
olla

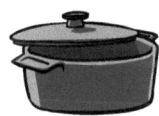

cast-iron pot
olla de fundición de hierro

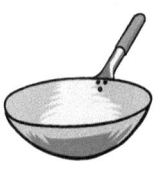

wok / kadai
wok / kadai

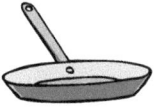

pan
sartén

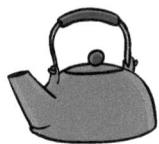

kettle
hervidor de agua

steamer

olla de vapor

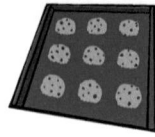

baking tray

bandeja de horno

crockery

vajilla

mug

vaso

bowl

bol

chopsticks

palillos para comer

ladle

cucharón de sopa

spatula

espátula

whisk

batidor

strainer

colador

sieve

cedazo

grater

rallador

mortar

mortero

barbecue

parrillada

fireplace

fogata

chopping board

tabla de picar

rolling pin

rodillo

corkscrew

sacacorchos

can

lata

can opener

abrelatas

oven cloth

agarrador

sink

fregadero

brush

cepillo

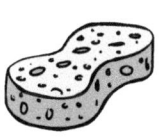

sponge

esponja

blender

batidora

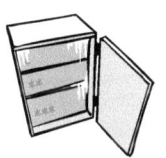

deep freezer

arcón congelador

baby bottle

biberón

tap

grifo

bathroom

cuarto de baño

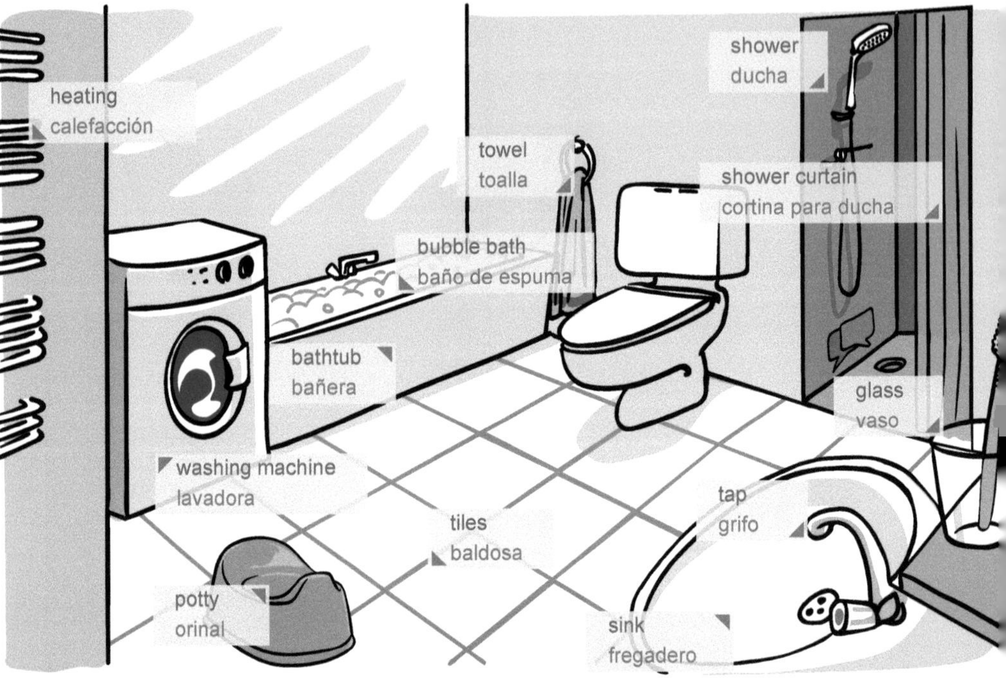
shower
ducha
heating
calefacción
towel
toalla
shower curtain
cortina para ducha
bubble bath
baño de espuma
bathtub
bañera
glass
vaso
washing machine
lavadora
tap
grifo
tiles
baldosa
potty
orinal
sink
fregadero

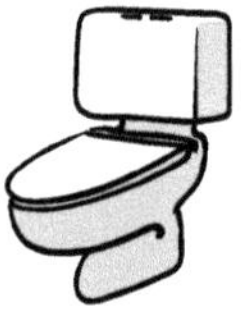

toilet

cuarto de baño

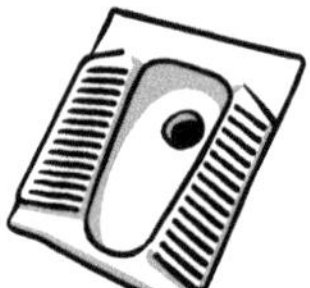

squat toilet

placa turca

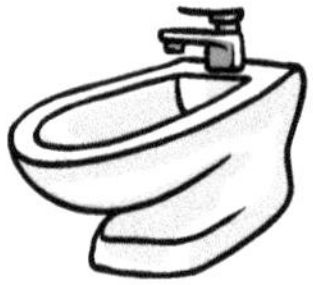

bidet

bidé

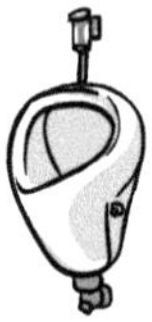

urinal

urinario

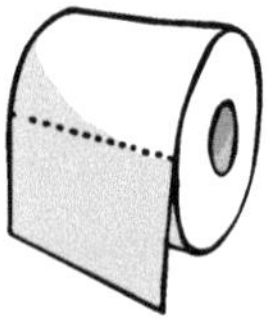

toilet paper

papel higiénico

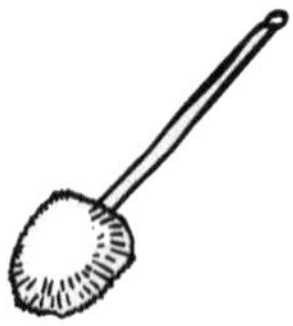

toilet brush

escobilla para el cuarto de baño

toothbrush

cepillo de dientes

toothpaste

pasta dentífrica

dental floss

seda dental

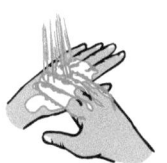

wash

lavar

hand shower

ducha teléfono

douche

ducha higiénica

basin

cuenco

back brush

cepillo para la espalda

soap

jabón

shower gel

gel de ducha

shampoo

champú

flannel

manopla para baño

drain

desagüe

creme

crema

deodorant

desodorante

mirror

espejo

hand mirror

espejo de maquillaje

razor

máquina de afeitar

shaving foam

espuma de afeitar

aftershave

loción para después del
afeitado

comb

peine

brush

cepillo

hair-dryer

secador para cabello

hairspray

laca de peinado

makeup

maquillaje

lipstick

lápiz labial

nail varnish

laca para uñas

cotton wool

algodón

nail scissors

tijera para uñas

perfume

perfume

washbag

neceser

stool

taburete

weighing scales

balanza

bathrobe

bata de baño

rubber gloves

guantes de goma

tampon

tampón

sanitary towel

compresa

chemical toilet

wáter químico

kids room
cuarto de los niños

alarm clock
despertador
cuddly toy
animal de peluche
toy car
auto de juguete
rattle
sonajero
doll's house
casa de muñecas
present
obsequio

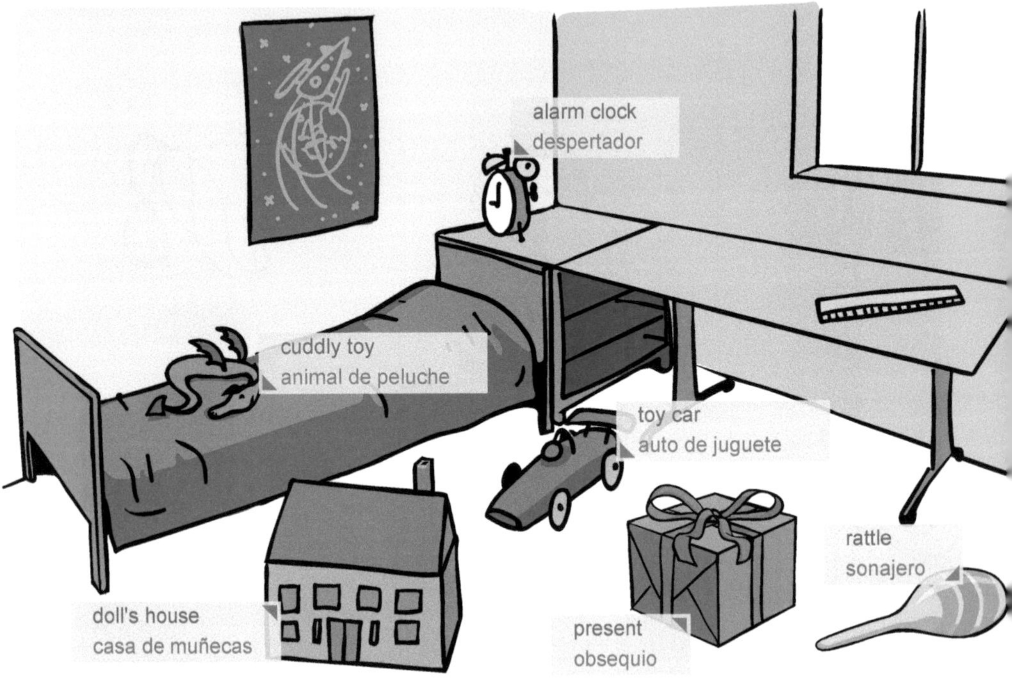

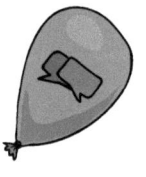

balloon

globo

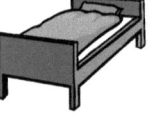

bed

cama

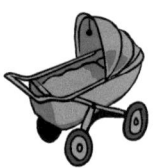

stroller

cochecito para niños

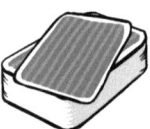

deck of cards

juego de barajas

jigsaw

rompecabezas

SUPER
MEGA

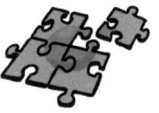

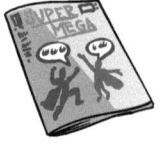

comic

cómic

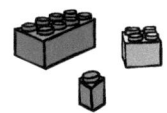

lego bricks

piezas de Lego

toy blocks

bloques para jugar

action figure

figura de acción

romper suit

pijama de una pieza

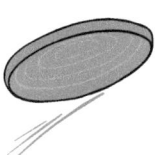

frisbee

frisbee

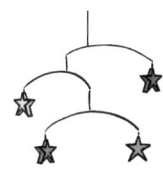

mobile

móvil

board game

juego de mesa

dice

dado

model train set

tren eléctrico a escala

pacifier

chupete

party

fiesta

picture book

libro de dibujos

ball

pelota

doll

títere

play

jugar

sandpit

arenero

swing

columpio

toys

juguetes

video game console

consola de videojuego

tricycle

triciclo

teddy bear

osito de peluche

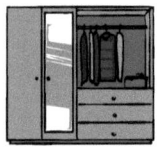

wardrobe

guardarropa

clothing

vestimenta

socks

calcetines

stockings

medias

tights

panti

scarf
chal

belt
cinturón

umbrella
paraguas

t-shirt
camiseta

sneakers
deportivas

boots
botas

slippers
zapatilla

sandals	shoes	rubber boots
sandalias	zapatos	botas de goma
underwear	bra	undershirt
ropa interior	corpiño	camiseta

body

body

pants

pantalón

jeans

jeans

skirt

falda

blouse

blusa

shirt

camisa

pullover

pullover

sweater

sweater

blazer

blazer

jacket

chaqueta

coat

abrigo

raincoat

impermeable

costume

traje chaqueta

dress

vestido

wedding dress

vestido de bodas

suit
traje

nightgown
camisón

pajamas
pijama

sari
sari

headscarf
pañuelo de cabeza

turban
turbante

burka
burka

kaftan
caftán

abaya
abaya

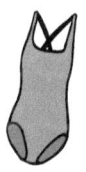

swimsuit
traje de baño

trunks
bañador

shorts
shorts

tracksuit
chándal

apron
delantal

gloves
guante

button

botón

glasses

gafa

bracelet

brazalete

necklace

cadena

ring

anillo

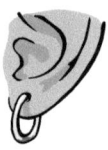

earring

aro

cap

gorra

coat hanger

percha

hat

sombrero

tie

corbata

zip

cierre a cremallera

helmet

casco

braces

tiradores

school uniform

uniforme escolar

uniform

uniforme

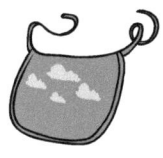

bib

babero

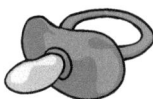

pacifier

chupete

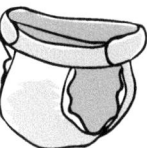

diaper

pañal

office

oficina

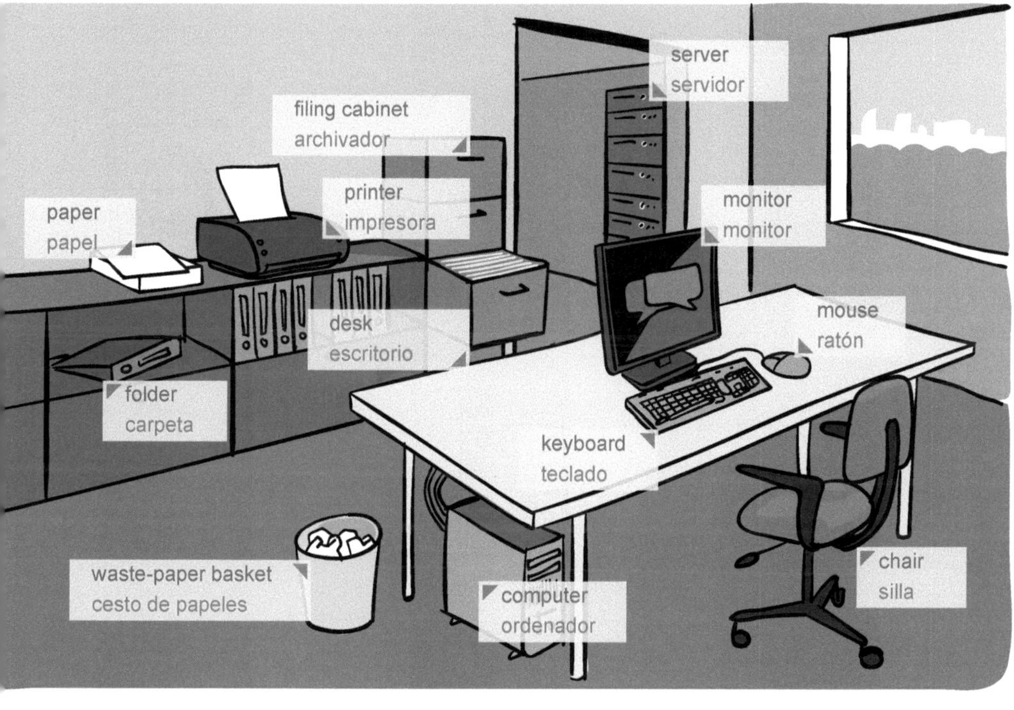
server
servidor
filing cabinet
archivador
printer
impresora
paper
papel
monitor
monitor
mouse
ratón
desk
escritorio
folder
carpeta
keyboard
teclado
waste-paper basket
cesto de papeles
computer
ordenador
chair
silla

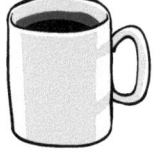

coffee mug

taza de café

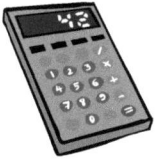

calculator

calculadora

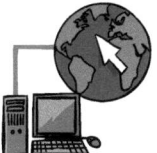

internet

internet

laptop

laptop

letter

carta

message

mensaje

cell phone

teléfono móvil

network

red

photocopier

fotocopiadora

software

software

telephone

teléfono

plug socket

tomacorriente

fax machine

máquina de fax

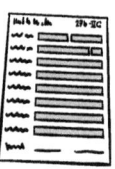

form

formulario

document

documento

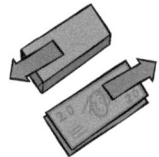

buy

comprar

pay

pagar

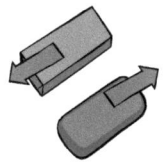

trade

comerciar

money

dinero

**USD**

dollar

dólar

**EUR**

euro

euro

**JPY**

yen

yen

**RUB**

rouble

rublo

**CHF**

Swiss franc

franco

**CNY**

renminbi yuan

renminbi

**INR**

rupee

rupia

cash point

cajero automático

currency exchange office

casa de cambio

gold

oro

silver

plata

oil

petróleo

energy

energía

price

precio

contract

contrato

tax

impuesto

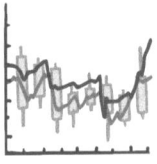

stock

acción

work

trabajar

employee

empleado

employer

empleador

factory

fábrica

shop

negocio

occupations
ocupaciones

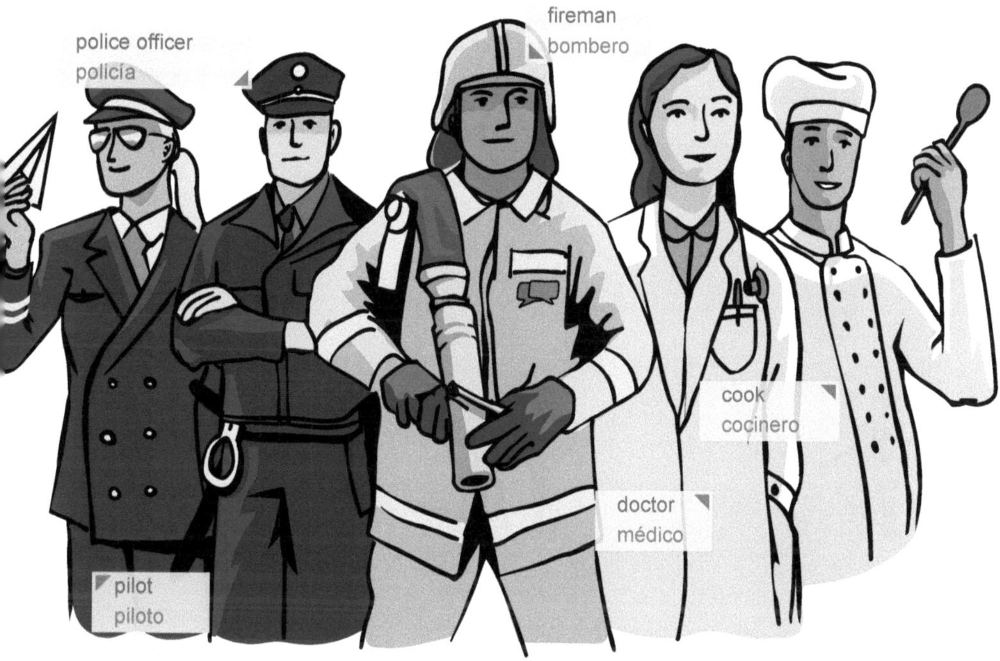

police officer
policía
fireman
bombero
cook
cocinero
doctor
médico
pilot
piloto

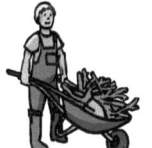

gardener

jardinero

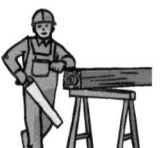

carpenter

carpintero

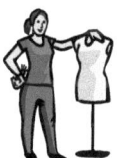

seamstress

costurera

judge

juez

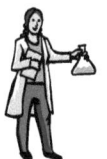

chemist

químico

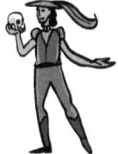

actor

actor

bus driver
conductor de autobús

taxi driver
taxista

fisherman
pescador

cleaning lady
mujer de la limpieza

roofer
techista

waiter
camarero

hunter
cazador

painter
pintor

baker
panadero

electrician
electricista

builder
albañil

engineer
ingeniero

butcher
carnicero

plumber
fontanero

postman
cartero

soldier

soldado

architect

arquitecto

cashier

cajero

florist

florista

hairdresser

peluquero

conductor

cobrador

mechanic

mecánico

captain

capitán

dentist

odontólogo

scientist

científico

rabbi

rabino

imam

imam

monk

monje

pastor

párroco

tools

herramientas

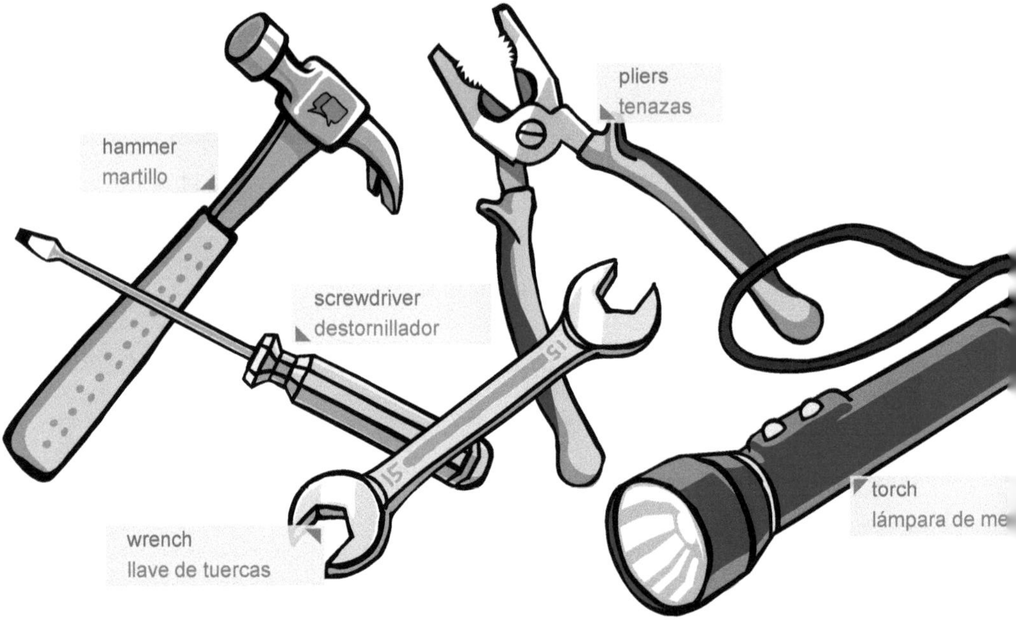
pliers
tenazas
hammer
martillo
screwdriver
destornillador
torch
lámpara de me
wrench
llave de tuercas

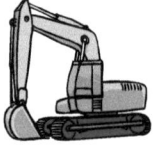

excavator

excavadora

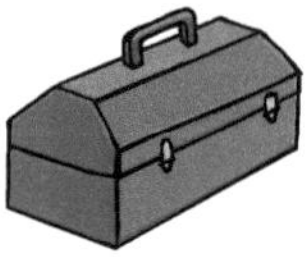

toolbox

caja de herramientas

ladder

escalerilla

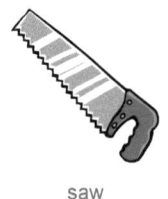

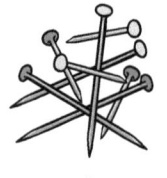

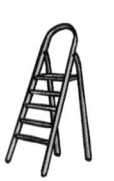

saw

serrucho

nails

clavos

drill

taladro

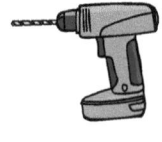

repair

reparar

shovel

pala

Damn!

¡Maldición!

dustpan

recogedor

paint can

lata de pintura

screws

tornillos

musical instruments
instrumentos musicales

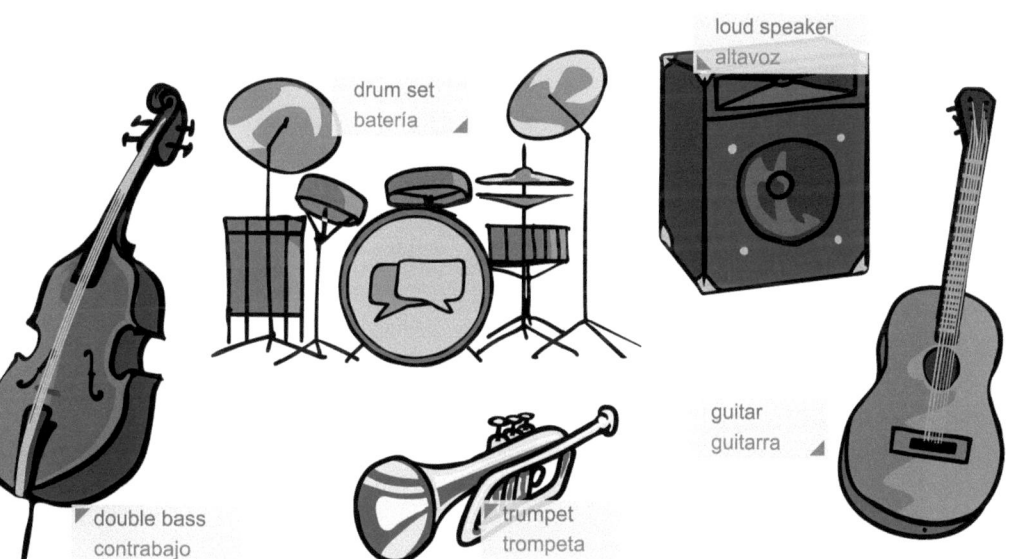

loud speaker
altavoz

drum set
batería

guitar
guitarra

double bass
contrabajo

trumpet
trompeta

piano

piano

violin

violín

bass

bajo

timpani

timbales

drums

tambor

keyboard

teclado

saxophone

saxofón

flute

flauta

microphone

micrófono

musical instruments - instrumentos musicales

zoo
zoológico

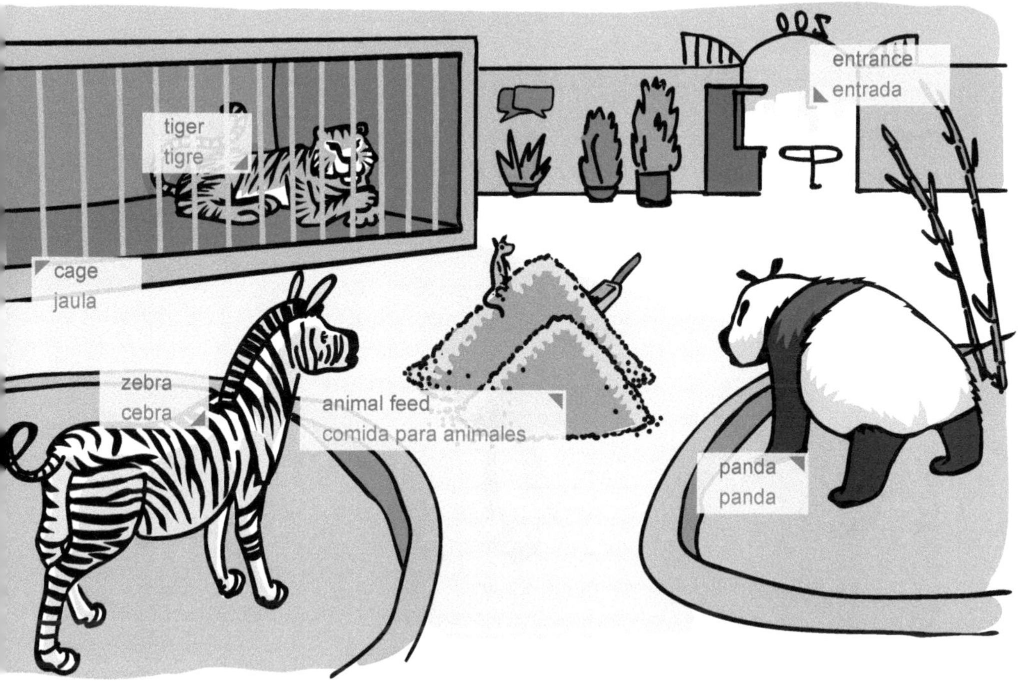

ZOO
entrance
entrada
tiger
tigre
cage
jaula
zebra
cebra
animal feed
comida para animales
panda
panda

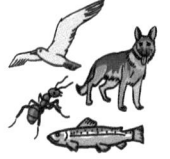

animals
animales

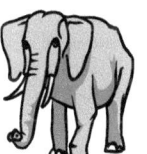

elephant
elefante

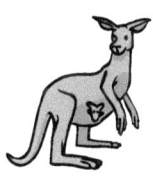

kangaroo
canguro

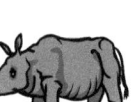

rhino
rinoceronte

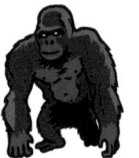

gorilla
gorila

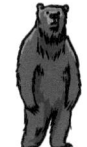

bear
oso

camel

camello

ostrich

avestruz

lion

león

monkey

mono

flamingo

flamengo

parrot

papagayo

polar bear

oso polar

penguin

pingüino

shark

tiburón

peacock

pavo real

snake

serpiente

crocodile

cocodrilo

zookeeper

cuidador del zoológico

seal

foca

jaguar

jaguar

zoo - zoológico

pony
pony

leopard
leopardo

hippo
hipopótamo

giraffe
jirafa

eagle
águila

boar
jabalí

fish
pescado

turtle
tortuga

walrus
morsa

fox
zorro

gazelle
gacela

American football
fútbol americano

cycling
ciclismo

tennis
tenis

basketball
baloncesto

swimming
natación

ice hockey
hockey sobre hielo

boxing
boxeo

soccer
fútbol

badminton
badminton

athletics
atletismo

handball
balonmano

skiing
esquí

polo
polo

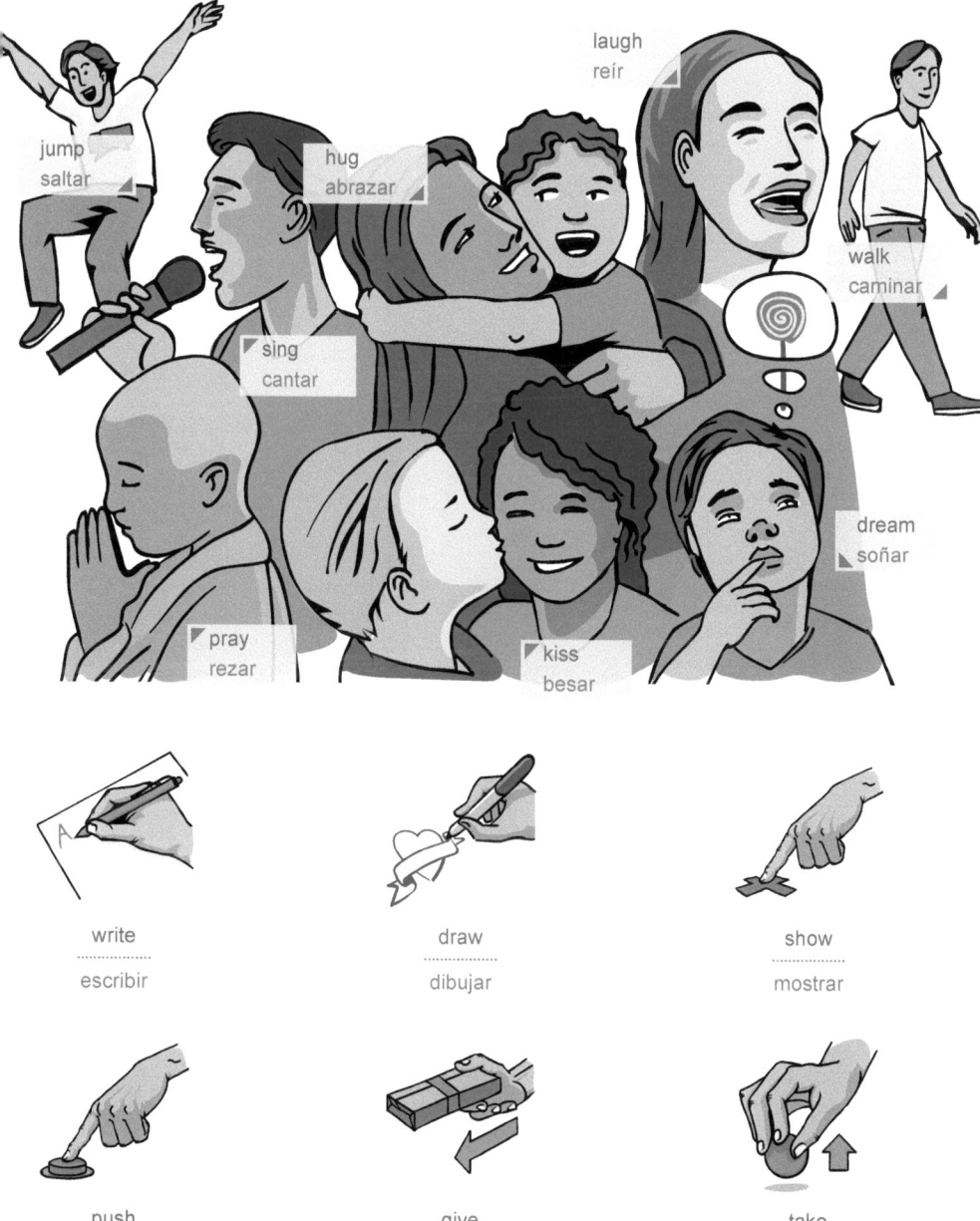

jump
saltar

laugh
reír

hug
abrazar

walk
caminar

sing
cantar

dream
soñar

pray
rezar

kiss
besar

write	draw	show
escribir	dibujar	mostrar

push	give	take
presionar	dar	tomar

have
tener

do
hacer

be
ser

stand
estar de pie

run
correr

pull
tirar

throw
arrojar

fall
caer

lie
estar acostado

wait
esperar

carry
llevar

sit
estar sentado

get dressed
vestirse

sleep
dormir

wake up
despertar

look at

mirar

cry

llorar

stroke

acariciar

comb

peinarse

talk

conversar

understand

entender

ask

preguntar

listen

oír

drink

beber

eat

comer

tidy up

asear

love

amar

cook

cocinar

drive

conducir

fly

volar

sail

navegar

calculate

calcular

read

leer

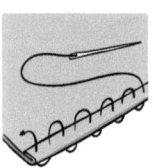

learn

aprender

work

trabajar

marry

casarse

sew

coser

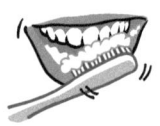

brush teeth

limpiarse los dientes

kill

matar

smoke

fumar

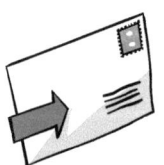

send

enviar

activities - actividades

grandmother
abuela

grandfather
abuelo

father
padre

mother
madre

baby
bebé

daughter
hija

son
hijo

guest

invitado

aunt

tía

uncle

tío

brother

hermano

sister

hermana

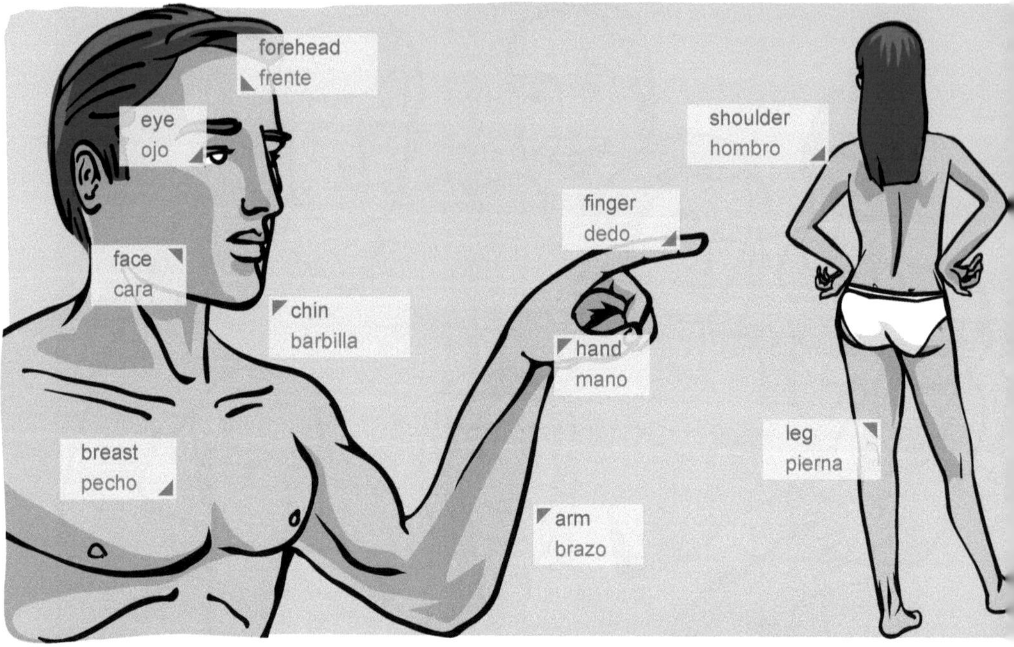

forehead
frente

eye
ojo

shoulder
hombro

finger
dedo

face
cara

chin
barbilla

hand
mano

breast
pecho

leg
pierna

arm
brazo

baby

bebé

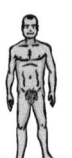

man

hombre

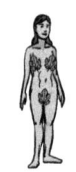

woman

mujer

girl

muchacha

boy

joven

head

cabeza

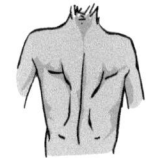

back

espalda

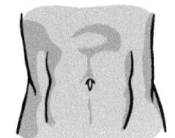

belly

vientre

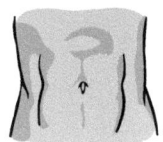

navel

ombligo

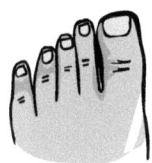

toe

dedo del pie

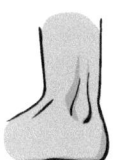

heel

talón

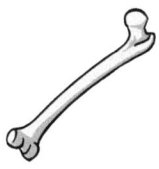

bone

hueso

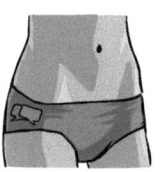

hip

cadera

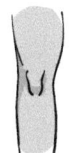

knee

rodilla

elbow

codo

nose

nariz

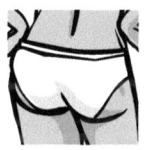

buttocks

trasero

skin

piel

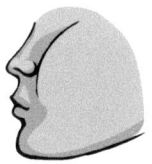

cheek

mejilla

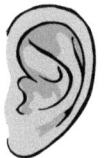

ear

oreja

lip

labio

body - cuerpo

mouth

boca

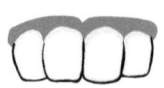

tooth

diente

tongue

lengua

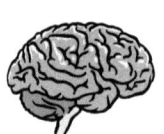

brain

cerebro

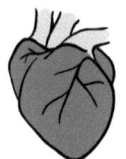

heart

corazón

muscle

músculo

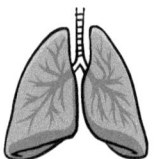

lung

pulmón

liver

hígado

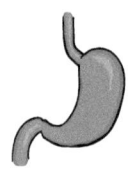

stomach

estómago

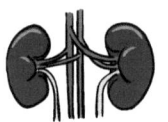

kidneys

riñones

sex

relación sexual

condom

condón

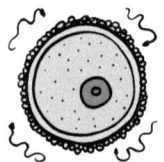

ovum

Óvulo

semen

esperma

pregnancy

embarazo

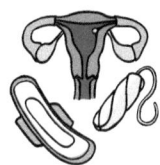

menstruation

menstruación

vagina

vagina

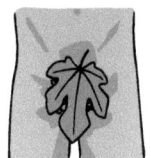

penis

pene

eyebrow

ceja

hair

cabello

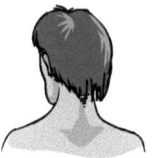

neck

cuello

hospital
hospital

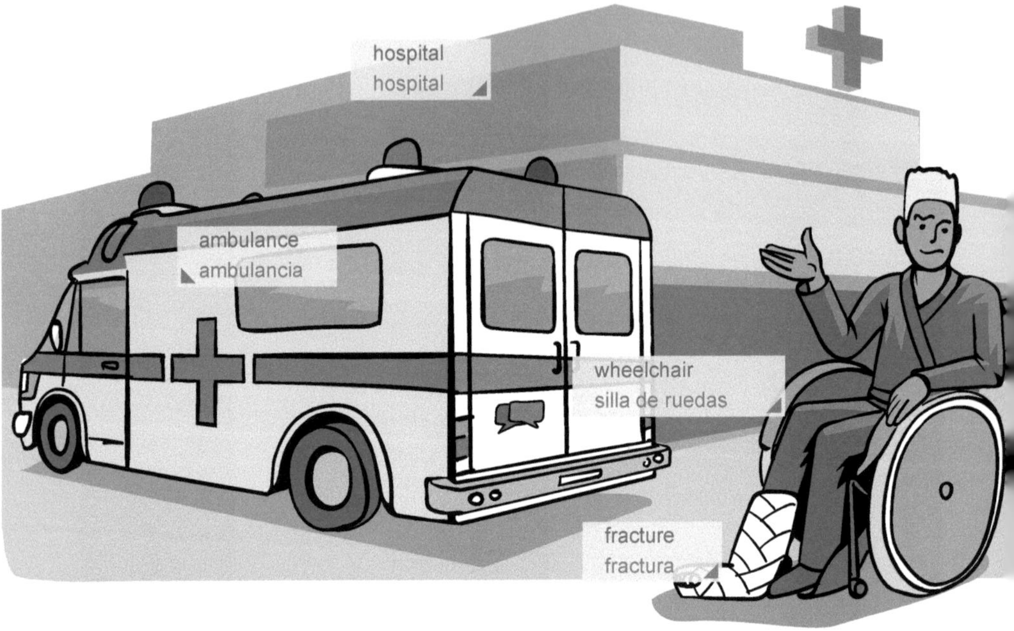

hospital
hospital
ambulance
ambulancia
wheelchair
silla de ruedas
fracture
fractura

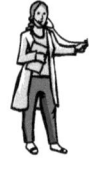

doctor

médico

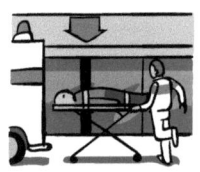

emergency room

admisión de urgencia

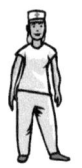

nurse

enfermera

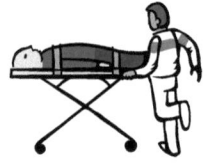

emergency

emergencia

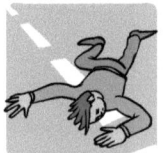

unconscious

inconsciente

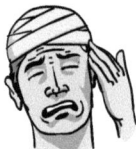

pain

dolor

injury

lesión

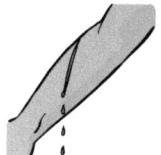

bleeding

hemorragia

heart attack

infarto de miocardio

stroke

apoplejía cerebral

allergy

alergia

cough

tos

fever

fiebre

flu

gripe

diarrhea

diarrea

headache

dolor de cabeza

cancer

cáncer

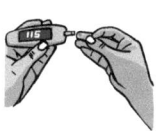

diabetes

diabetes

surgeon

cirujano

scalpel

escalpelo

operation

operación

hospital - hospital

CT

TC

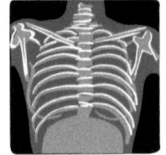

x-ray

rayos X

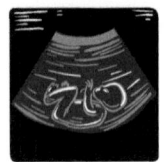

ultrasound

ultrasonido

face mask

máscara

disease

enfermedad

waiting room

sala de espera

crutch

muleta

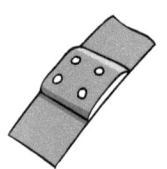

plaster

emplasto

bandage

vendaje

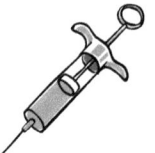

injection

inyección

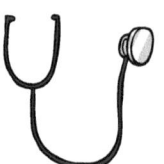

stethoscope

estetoscopio

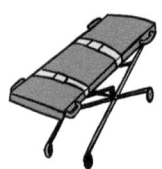

stretcher

camilla

clinical thermometer

termómetro

birth

nacimiento

overweight

sobrepeso

hospital - hospital

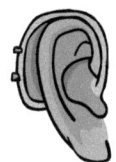

hearing aid

audífono

disinfectant

desinfectante

infection

infección

virus

virus

HIV / AIDS

VIH / SIDA

medicine

medicina

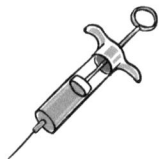

vaccination

vacunación

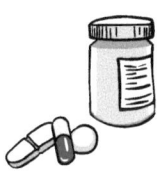

tablets

comprimido

pill

píldora anticonceptiva

emergency call

llamada de emergencia

blood pressure monitor

medidor de presión arterial

ill / healthy

enfermo / saludable

Help!

¡Ayuda!

alarm

alarma

assault

asalto

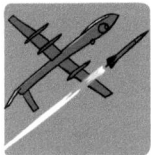

attack

ataque

danger

peligro

emergency exit

salida de emergencia

Fire!

¡Fuego!

fire extinguisher

extintor

accident

accidente

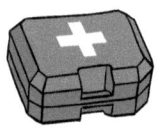

first-aid kit

kit de primeros auxilios

SOS

SOS

police

Policía

Europe

Europa

North America

América del Norte

South America

América del Sur

Africa

África

Asia

Asia

Australia

Australia

Atlantic

Atlántico

Pacific

Pacífico

Indian Ocean

Océano Índico

Antarctic Ocean

Océano Antártico

Arctic Ocean

Océano Ártico

North pole

Polo Norte

South pole

Polo Sur

Antarctica

Antártida

earth

Tierra

land

país

sea

mar

island

isla

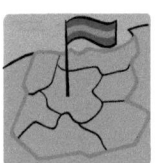

nation

nación

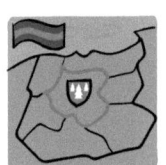

state

Estado

clock face

cuadrante

hour hand

horario

minute hand

minutero

second hand

segundero

What time is it?

¿Qué hora es?

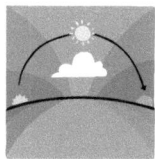

day

día

time

tiempo

now

ahora

digital watch

reloj digital

minute

minuto

hour

hora

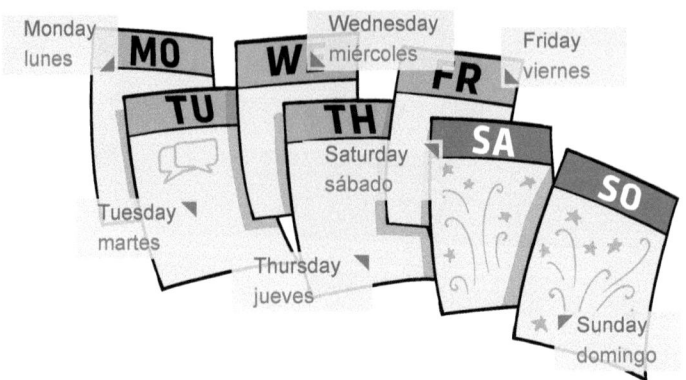

Monday
lunes

Wednesday
miércoles

Friday
viernes

Tuesday
martes

Saturday
sábado

Thursday
jueves

Sunday
domingo

yesterday

ayer

today

hoy

tomorrow

mañana

morning

mañana

noon

mediodía

evening

tarde

MO	TU	WE	TH	FR	SA	SU
1	2	3	4	5	6	7
8	9	10	11	12	13	14
15	16	17	18	19	20	21
22	23	24	25	26	27	28
29	30	31	1	2	3	4

workdays

jornada de trabajo

MO	TU	WE	TH	FR	SA	SU
1	2	3	4	5	6	7
8	9	10	11	12	13	14
15	16	17	18	19	20	21
22	23	24	25	26	27	28
29	30	31	1	2	3	4

weekend

fin de semana

year
año

rain
lluvia
spring
primavera
summer
verano
wind
viento
fall
otoño
snow
nieve
winter
invierno

4.APRIL 11°
5.APRIL 4°
6.APRIL 13°
7.APRIL 8°
8.APRIL 10°

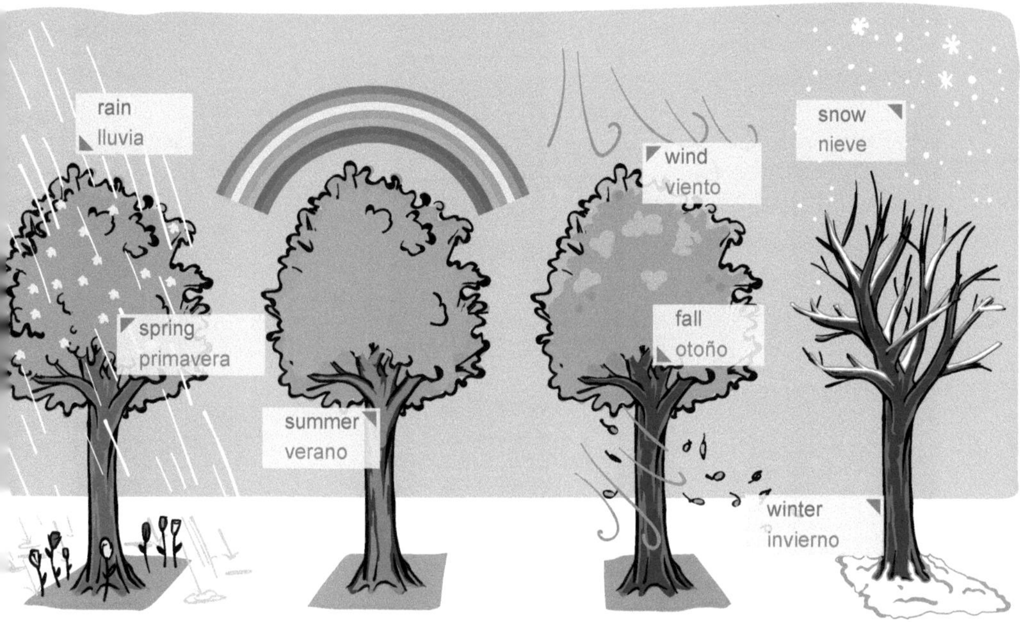

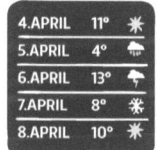

weather forecast

pronóstico meteorológico

F C
120 90 60 30 0 -30
40 30 20 10 0 -10 -20

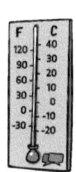

thermometer

termómetro

sunshine

luz solar

cloud

nube

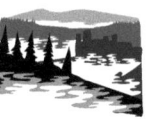

fog

niebla

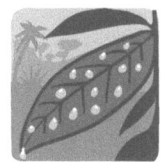

humidity

humedad ambiente

lightning

relámpago

thunder

trueno

storm

tormenta

hail

granizo

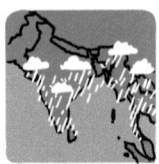

monsoon

monzón

flood

inundación

ice

hielo

January

enero

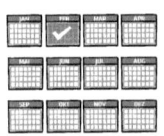

February

febrero

March

marzo

April

abril

May

mayo

June

junio

July

julio

August

agosto

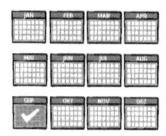

September
....
septiembre

October
....
octubre

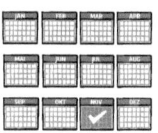

November
....
noviembre

December
....
diciembre

shapes
formas

circle
....
círculo

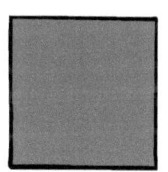

square
....
cuadrado

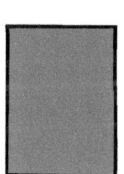

rectangle
....
rectángulo

triangle
....
triángulo

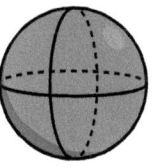

sphere
....
esfera

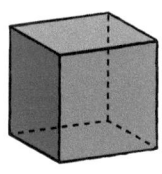

cube
....
cubo

white

blanco

yellow

amarillo

orange

anaranjado

pink

rosa

red

rojo

purple

lila

blue

azul

green

verde

brown

marrón

gray

gris

black

negro

a lot / a little

mucho / poco

angry / calm

enojado / calmado

beautiful / ugly

bonito / feo

beginning / end

comienzo / fin

big / small

grande / pequeño

bright / dark

claro / oscuro

brother / sister

hermano / hermana

clean / dirty

limpio / sucio

complete / incomplete

completo / incompleto

day / night

día / noche

dead / alive

muerto / vivo

wide / narrow

ancho / angosto

edible / inedible

disfrutable / no disfrutable

evil / kind

malo / amigable

excited / bored

excitado / aburrido

fat / thin

gordo / delgado

first / last

primero / último

friend / enemy

amigo / enemigo

full / empty

lleno / vacío

hard / soft

duro / suave

heavy / light

pesado / liviano

hunger / thirst

hambre / sed

ill / healthy

enfermo / saludable

illegal / legal

ilegal / legal

intelligent / stupid

inteligente / tonto

left / right

izquierda / derecha

near / far

cercano / lejano

new / used

nuevo / usado

nothing / something

nada / algo

old / young

viejo / joven

on / off

encendido / apagado

open / closed

abierto / cerrado

quiet / loud

bajo / fuerte

rich / poor

rico / pobre

right / wrong

correcto / incorrecto

rough / smooth

áspero / liso

sad / happy

triste / alegre

short / long

breve / extenso

slow / fast

lento / veloz

wet / dry

mojado / seco

warm / cool

caliente / frío

war / peace

guerra / paz

0

zero

cero

1

one

uno

2

two

dos

3

three

tres

4

four

cuatro

5

five

cinco

6

six

seis

7

seven

siete

8

eight

ocho

9

nine

nueve

10

ten

diez

11

eleven

once

12
twelve

doce

13
thirteen

trece

14
fourteen

catorce

15
fifteen

quince

16
sixteen

dieciséis

17
seventeen

diecisiete

18
eighteen

dieciocho

19
nineteen

diecinueve

20
twenty

veinte

100
hundred

cien

1.000
thousand

mil

1.000.000
million

millón

languages
idiomas

English
....
inglés

American English
....
inglés estadounidense

Chinese Mandarin
....
chino mandarín

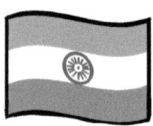

Hindi
....
hindi

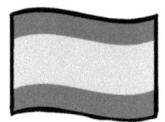

Spanish
....
español

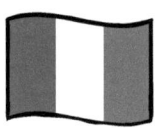

French
....
francés

Arabic
....
árabe

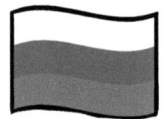

Russian
....
ruso

Portuguese
....
portugués

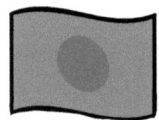

Bengali
....
bengalí

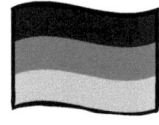

German
....
alemán

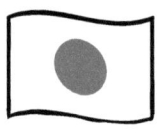

Japanese
....
japonés

I
....
yo

you
....
tú

he / she / it
....
él / ella

we
....
nosotros

you
....
vosotros

they
....
ellos

who?
....
¿quién?

what?
....
¿qué?

how?
....
¿cómo?

where?
....
¿dónde?

when?
....
¿cuándo?

name
....
nombre

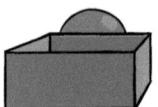

behind

detrás

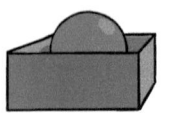

in

en

in front of

delante de

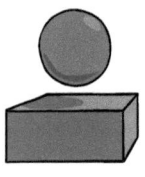

over

encima de

on

sobre

under

debajo de

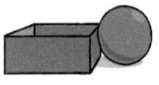

beside

junto a

between

entre

place

lugar